Contents

Teachers' notes	1	Windows	17
Guinea pigs	5	Dotty toys	18
Teddies	6	Elephant counting cards	21
More teddies	7	Stars	22
Teddy cut-outs	8	Elephants in order	23
Lorry counting cards	9	Tub games	24
Using the counting cards	10	Parent's letter	27
Boxes	11	Tub sums – 1	28
Big and small – 1	12	Tub sums – 2	29
Big and small – 2	13	Tub sums – 3	30
0 to 9 ant cards	14	Birds	31
0 to 9 number cards	15	More birds	32
Calculator number cards	16		

Teachers' notes

Aim of this book
The aim of this book is to provide you with well-presented and mathematically valuable material which will link with your existing schemes of work for mathematics and which children will also enjoy using.

To help you make the best use of the activities, please read the notes which follow.

Printing
Although photocopying the sheets on to white paper may be the simplest way of reproducing the activities in this book, do consider other alternatives. Some pages benefit from copying directly on to coloured paper or card. If your school does not have the necessary equipment, you may be able to use the printing facilities of a larger primary school, a secondary school or a teachers' centre.

To keep re-usable cards and worksheets in good condition, put them inside plastic wallets, laminate them or cover them with clear adhesive plastic film. Even copies made on paper can be surprisingly strong when covered.

Record-keeping and storage
We have not provided a separate system of record-keeping for these activities, as most teachers prefer to add to their existing scheme of records. You could use the child's own maths writing book to make a note of activities used, when this would be helpful information to have. Worksheets can usually be fastened into the child's book like an extra page by using a piece of adhesive tape at the side, and act as an obvious reminder of an activity completed.

Mathematical context
This book provides activities to help children with counting objects, counting forwards and backwards, reading and writing numbers, putting numbers in order, using ordinal numbers (ie 1st, 2nd, 3rd and so on) and carrying out simple additions and subtractions in context. Children are encouraged to use a calculator too, as calculators provide a strong motive for them to learn and use the numerals 0 to 9, and the symbols +, - and =. Written work is linked to practical activity, and children are given the opportunity to make up questions and problems for each other.

Every activity needs introducing by the teacher if the children are to make the most of it. A few moments spent discussing their work once they have finished is also obviously worthwhile. Sometimes activities may be taken home by the children to share with their families.

Although the title of this book is *Numbers to 9*, you will find that as children grow in confidence they will extend many of the activities to use larger numbers.

Notes on individual activities

Page 5: Guinea pigs

Use the sheet of guinea pigs for children to make their own 'counting picture', for which either you or they could write a caption. Green sugar paper, cut to about A3 size, will make a good background. Talk about how many guinea pigs the child wants to stick on. Will they be in a hutch or out in the grass? Children who can confidently count more than six might like to draw a few guinea pigs of their own, to add to their picture.

Pages 6 and 7: Teddies and More teddies

Stuck together, these two sheets make a line of seven teddies under flaps, so that you can count forwards (none, 1, 2, 3, 4, 5, 6, 7) and backwards, as well as lifting flaps more randomly and counting up how many teddies you can see altogether.

The children may enjoy singing 'Seven little teddies sitting on a wall' to the tune of 'Ten green bottles', as they close down the flaps one by one.

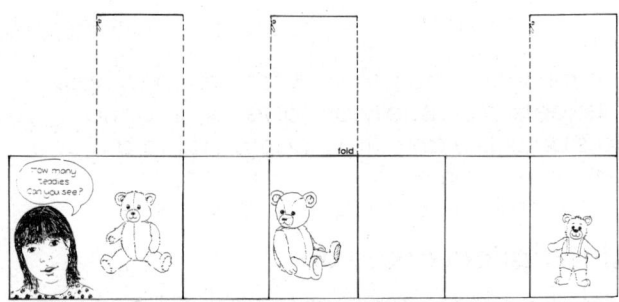

Page 8: Teddy cut-outs

The children could stick the teddies on to a collage background, such as a garden or a party. Write a caption for the picture, such as '9 teddies in the park'.

Pages 9 to 13: Lorries

The lorry counting cards provide a simple but very effective way of practising counting and simple sums.

Use page 9 to make the equipment.
- Make four copies of the page on card, to make eight lorry cards. Alternatively, print copies on paper then mount them on card.
- Colour the lorries and their drivers. Use different colours for each card if you wish.
- Trim each card to fit a suitable storage box (for example, a 2-litre ice-cream tub or a large sandwich box). Cover each card with clear adhesive plastic film. Label the box and lid with photocopies of the labels below.
- Make between 80 and 100 'boxes' to use as counters on the lorries, by cutting out rectangles of thick card in a variety of sizes and colours (see the boxes drawn on the lorries on page 12 as examples). Alternatively, use big and small lolly sticks to represent timber or use your own or the children's ideas for cargo.

Make 'Lorry books' for the children by copying page 9 on to paper, then trimming the top and bottom of the pages along the dotted lines, and

◆ ESSENTIALS FOR MATHS: Numbers to 9

cutting along the centre where indicated. Do not trim off the left-hand side.

Use these sheets for children's own recording. Initially, they may draw on boxes, count them, and then you write the number on their sheet for them. Later, they can write the number themselves.

Use one sheet as a front cover and staple together several sheets of the child's work, to make their 'Lorry Book'.

Page 10 can be printed back-to-back with itself to make two A5 copies of notes on some initial activities to try. Keep a copy of these notes in each box of equipment as a reminder to adults or older children, who are helping by giving extra counting practice.

Once children are familiar with the counting cards, they can usually work without adult supervision for quite a while.

Pages 11, 12 and 13 provide further linked work. Children may benefit from using several copies of page 13, or you may want them to use plain paper to make up their own pictorial sums. The elephant counting cards on pages 21 to 23 can be used in a similar way to the lorries; there are also sets of counting cards in another book in this series, *Numbers to 20*.

Pages 14 to 16: 0 to 9 cards

Copy these three pages on to card, preferably using three different colours, then cut them out. Use just the 0 to 5 cards at first, then 0 to 9.

You will probably think of several ways in which you can use them, but here are a few suggestions:
• Putting them in order: shuffle one set of cards. Can the child to lay them out in order, smallest to largest, or vice versa?
• Matching: shuffle two sets of cards. Can the child match the ant cards to the correct numerals, or the standard numbers to the calculator numbers? (Provide a calculator to let the child check these by pressing each key in turn).

• Snap: use two or three sets of cards shuffled together to play this traditional game.

The number cards can also be used with the lorry and elephant counting cards (pages 9 to 13 and 21 to 23), and with the tub games (pages 24 to 30).

Page 17: Windows

Children can use this worksheet on its own, colouring in each group of figures and writing the correct number by the side of each window (not forgetting 0).

Alternatively, print copies of page 15 on paper, to cut up and put the correct number over each window. Fasten each number with a piece of sticky tape down the left-hand edge, to make a flap which you can open to see the children again.

Pages 18 to 20: Dotty toys

These pages make six A5 dot-to-dot worksheets, each starting with zero. Make sure that the children realise they should join the dots, not the numbers. Dot-to-dots are a good way to practise recognising numerals in order.

Pages 21 to 23: Elephants

The elephant counting cards can be used in similar ways to the lorry counting cards (on pages 9 to 13). Make the cards in the same way (see page 2). Colour the elephants, but leave their blankets plain so that counters will show up clearly on them. Buttons, sequins, pasta wheels or small pieces of felt can be used as counters. Store the cards in a box, using the photocopiable labels above. Include a copy of the notes from page 10 in the box.

Encourage the children to arrange their decorations on the elephants' blankets in patterns if they can. You can emphasise traditional arrangements, like ⁙ for five, or they can make up their own.

Make 'Elephant books' for the children in the same way as the 'Lorry books' described earlier.

◆ ESSENTIALS FOR MATHS: Numbers to 9

Alternatively, glue several sheets end to end to make a frieze or to fold into a zig-zag book.

Pages 22 and 23 provide further linked work. Page 22 may be used with adhesive paper stars, or you may prefer the children to draw their own. Choose your own number of stars for each elephant. Page 23 looks at the first three ordinal numbers; if you make an elephant frieze you could extend this idea.

Pages 24 to 30: Tub games

Print pages 24, 25 and 26 on card, then cut them in half where indicated. This set of six cards describes a group of progressively more challenging practical activities which also help develop skills in mental arithmetic. Introduce each activity yourself, then leave the card as a reminder to the group who are playing.

Children's progress in learning number bonds will be much faster if you can involve older pupils, or parents or other members of their families, in playing the games. Use the letter on page 27 to send home, and copy pages 24 to 26 on to paper, cut them in two and staple them together along the left-hand side to make a booklet to accompany the letter. A set of 0 – 9 cards (page 15) should also be included.

The worksheet on page 28 provides a model for the children to follow to make their own sums for friends to try, using copies of pages 29 and 30. Make sure that children have the tubs and counters available to use as they make up their own sums. The children soon discover (because their friends tell them!) how important it is to write numbers carefully if they want other people to be able to read them; it is a powerful incentive for children to improve their handwriting.

Pages 31 and 32: Birds and More birds

These pages provide a simple story about subtraction. Once children have completed 'Birds' successfully, they can use copies of 'More Birds' either individually, or working with friends to make up problems for each other.

National Curriculum: Maths

In addition to the relevant programmes of study in AT1, the following PoS from AT2 are relevant to the activities in this book:

Level 1
* counting, reading, writing and ordering numbers to at least 10.
* learning that the size of a set is given by the last number in the count.
* understanding the language associated with number, eg 'more', 'fewer', 'the same'.
* understanding the conservation of number.
* making a sensible estimate of a number of objects up to 10.
* using addition and subtraction, with numbers no greater than 10, in the context of real objects.

Level 2
* knowing and using addition and subtraction facts up to 10.
* solving whole-number problems involving addition and subtraction.
* comparing two numbers to find the difference.

Some of the activities in this book may also be useful for work on AT3 programmes of study.

Scottish 5 – 14 Curriculum: Mathematics

Attainment outcome	Strand	Attainment target	Level
Number, money and measurement	Range and type of number	Work with numbers 0 to 20 (count, order, read/ write statements, display on calculator).	A
	Add and subtract	Add and subtract mentally for numbers 0 to 10.	A

Scottish Attainment Target chart compiled by Margaret Scott and Susan Gow

◆ Name _____

Guinea pigs

◆ Colour the guinea pigs. Cut them out. Use them to make a picture of your own.

ESSENTIALS FOR MATHS: Numbers to 9

◆ Name _____

Teddies

◆ Colour the teddies. Cut along the dotted lines to the middle of the sheet.

Cut this section out completely.

ESSENTIALS FOR MATHS: Numbers to 9

◆ Name _____

More teddies

◆ Colour the teddies. Glue the bottom of this sheet under the top line of page 6, to make seven teddies in a line.

◆ ESSENTIALS FOR MATHS: Numbers to 9

◆ Name _____

Teddy cut-outs

◆ Colour the teddies. Cut them out. Use them to make a picture of your own. Draw extra teddies if you want to.

◆ ESSENTIALS FOR MATHS: Numbers to 9

Lorry counting cards

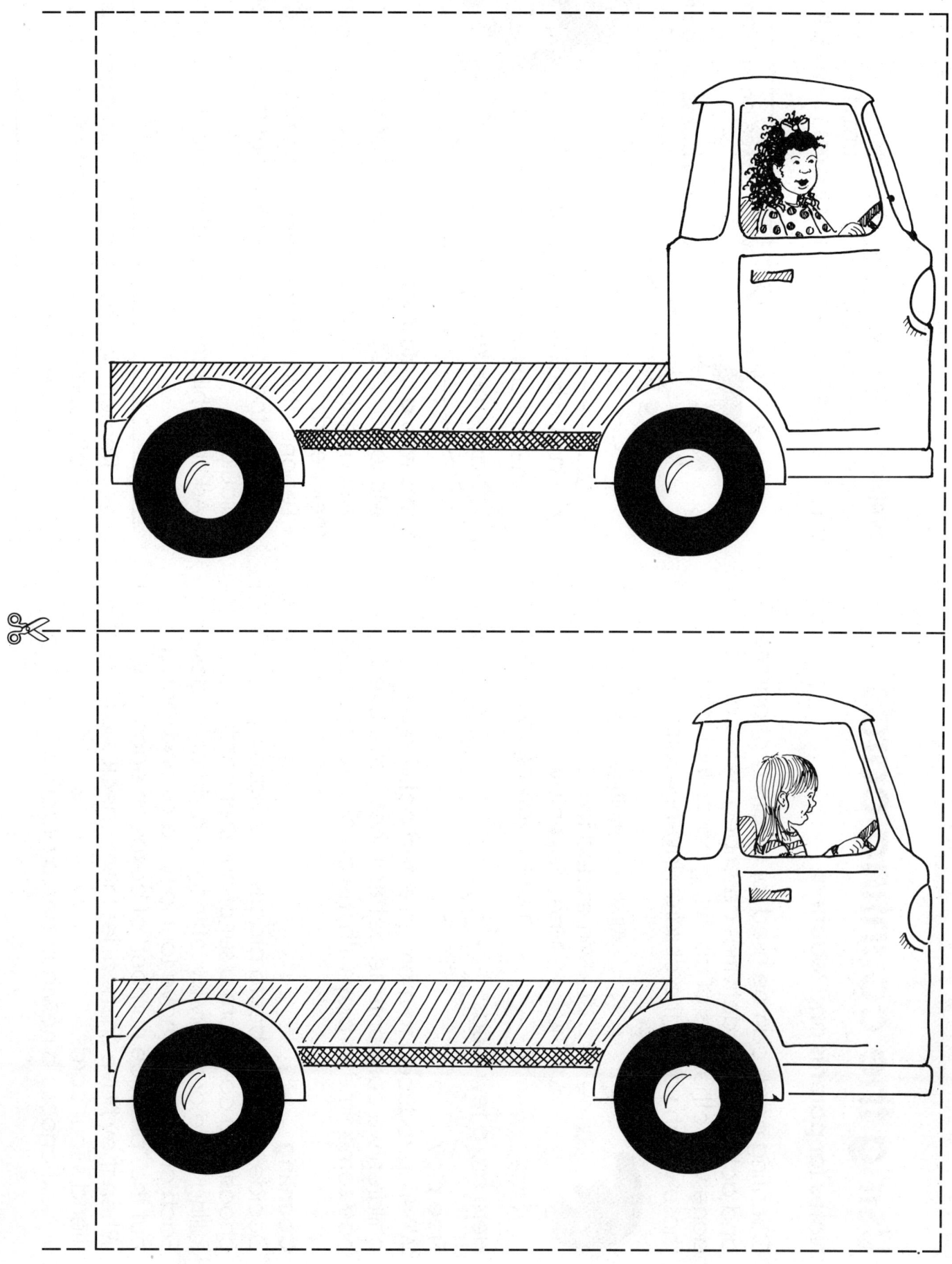

◆ ESSENTIALS FOR MATHS: Numbers to 9

Simple sums

Ask the pairs to make up some sums for each other and then use the lorries and boxes to work them out.

I put 5 boxes on my lorry then I put on 2 more. How many boxes are on my lorry, altogether?

I had 8 boxes on my lorry. Then I took 4 off. How many boxes are left on the lorry?

Sums with a calculator

- Make up a sum like the ones above.
- Ask both children to try to work out the sum in their heads.
- Let one child use the lorries and boxes to work it out while the other child works out the sum on a calculator.

Ask the children to swap over for the next sum.

Remember that short, frequent periods of counting are more useful than long, infrequent sessions.

Using the counting cards
Notes for parents and teachers

Counting cards can be used for a variety of games and activities. The activities described here can be done with other sets of counting cards, including those which you or the children invent yourselves.

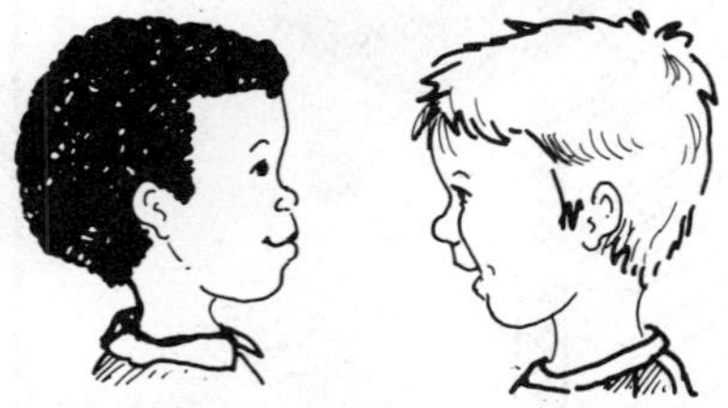

Here are a few ideas:

All the activities are intended to be undertaken by two children working together.

Free play

When introduced to more directed activities, children will concentrate better if they have already had some time to play with the cards and counters.

Counting

Decide on a number to practise, perhaps by choosing a card from a set of number cards, by rolling a die or simply by letting the children choose. Each child should have four lorry cards and should put the 'practice number' of boxes on each lorry. When they have finished, let them check their friend's four cards.
Next choose a new number to practise.

◆ ESSENTIALS FOR MATHS: Numbers to 9

◆ Name ───────────

Boxes

◆ Colour in the boxes. How many boxes are on each lorry?

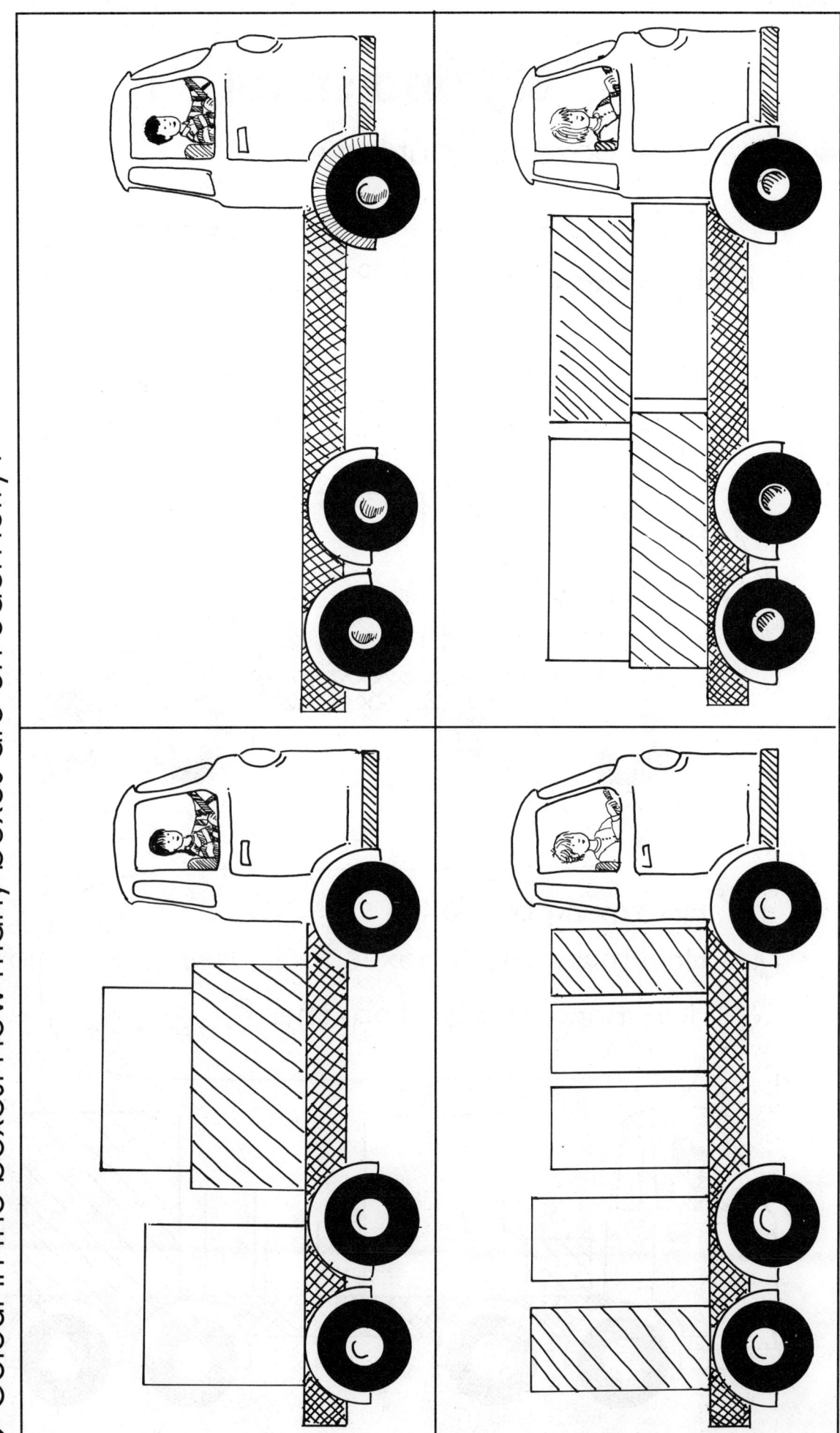

◆ ESSENTIALS FOR MATHS: Numbers to 9

◆ Name _____

Big and small – 1

◆ Count the boxes on our lorries.

How many big boxes? ....
How many small boxes? ....
How many boxes altogether? ....

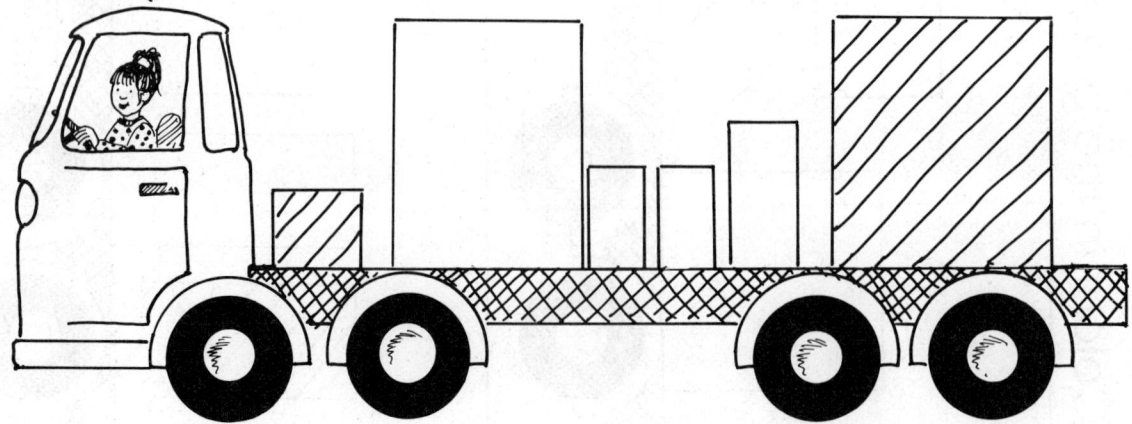

How many big boxes? ....
How many small boxes? ....
How many boxes altogether? ....

◆ Name _____

Big and small – 2

◆ Draw some big and small boxes on the lorry.

How many big boxes? ....
How many small boxes? ....
How many boxes altogether? ....

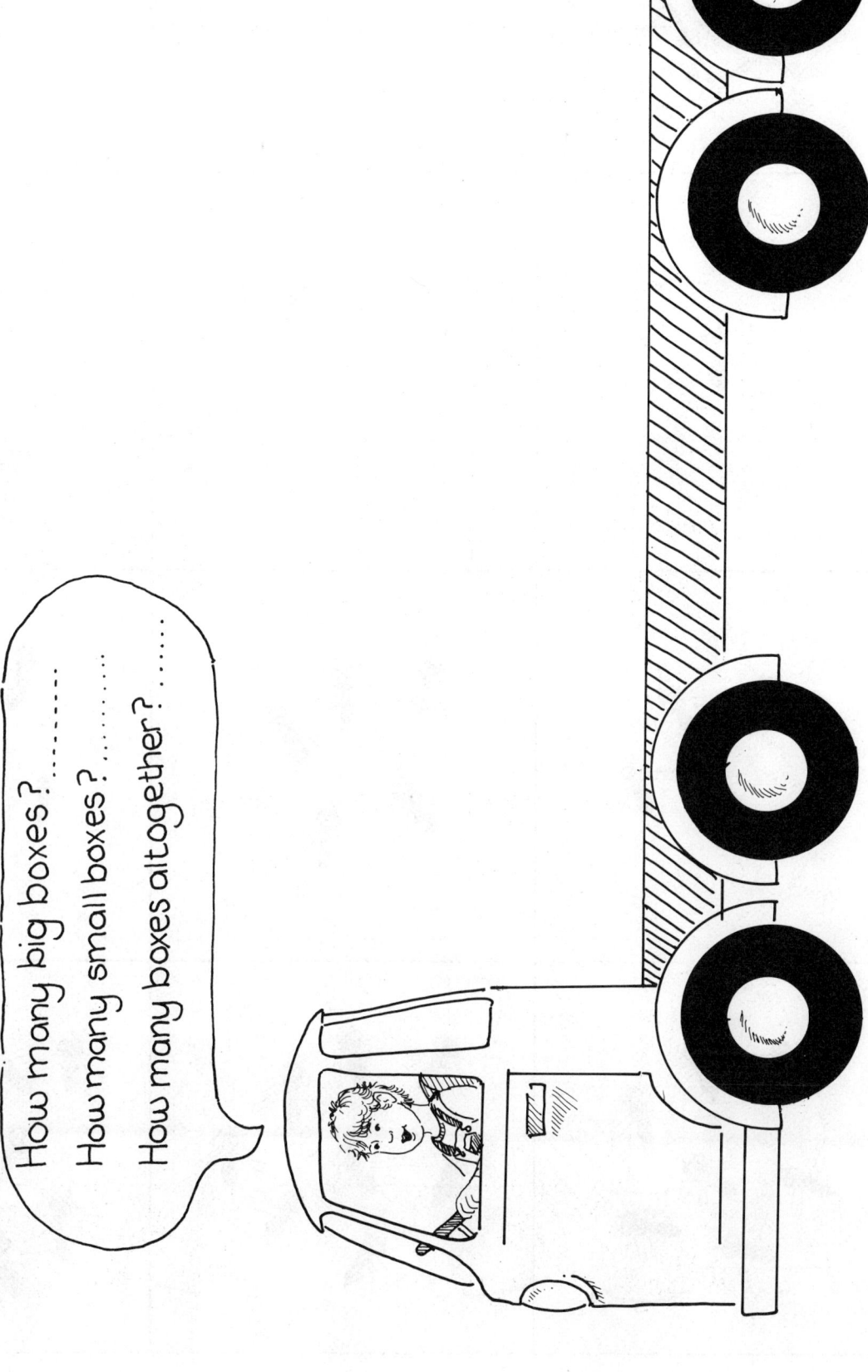

◆ ESSENTIALS FOR MATHS: Numbers to 9

13

0 to 9 ant cards

◆ Cut out the ten cards.

◆ ESSENTIALS FOR MATHS: Numbers to 9

0 to 9 number cards

◆ Cut out the number cards. Make sure that the solid band is along the bottom of each card.

0

1	2	3

4	5	6

7	8	9

◆ ESSENTIALS FOR MATHS: Numbers to 9

Calculator number cards

◆ Cut out the cards. Make sure that the solid band is along the bottom of each card.

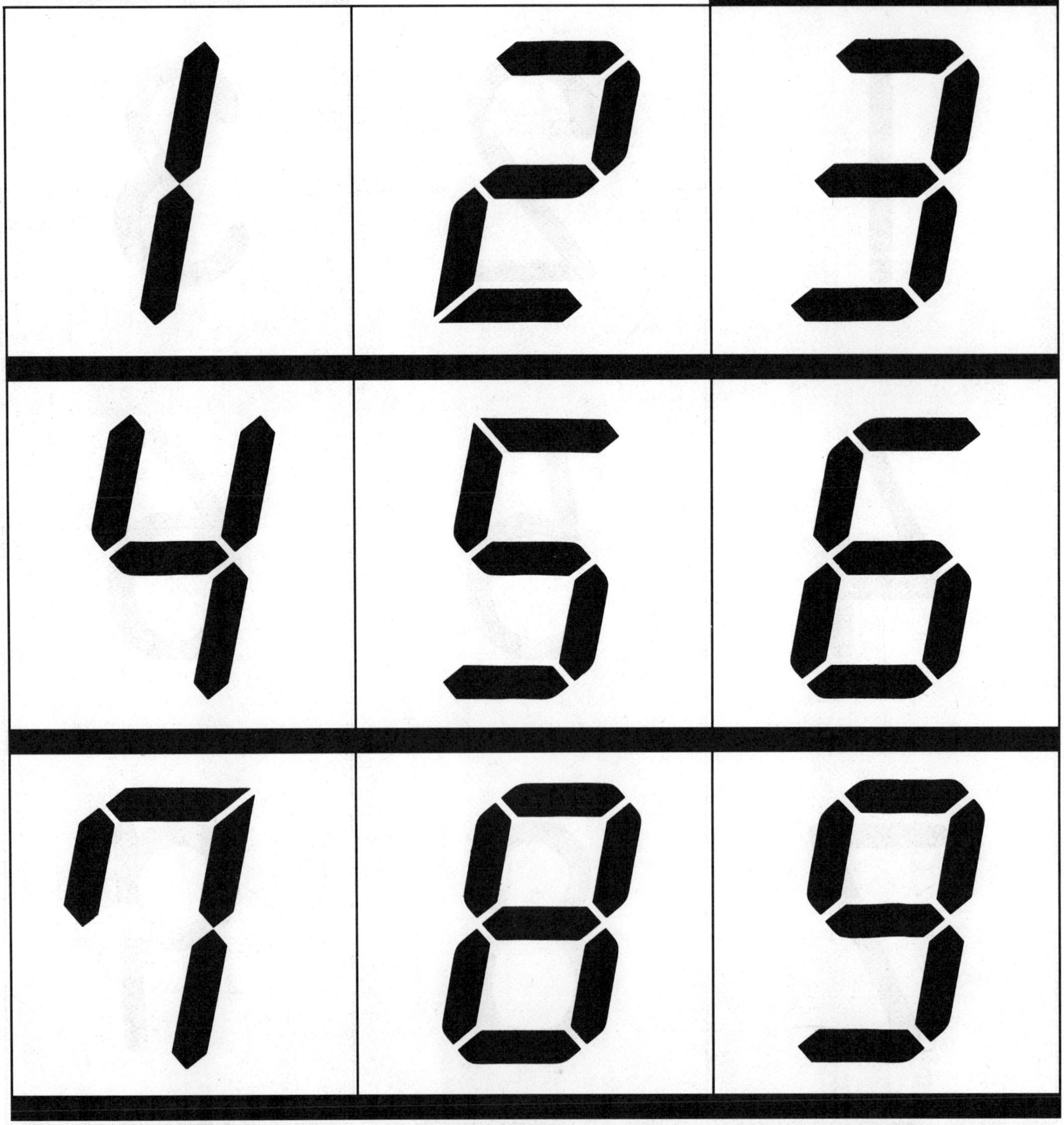

ESSENTIALS FOR MATHS: Numbers to 9   16

◆ Name _____

Windows

◆ How many children are looking out of each window?

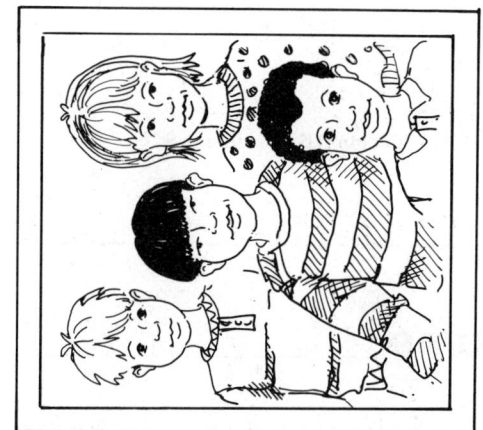

◆ ESSENTIALS FOR MATHS: Numbers to 9

◆ Name _____

Dotty toys – 1

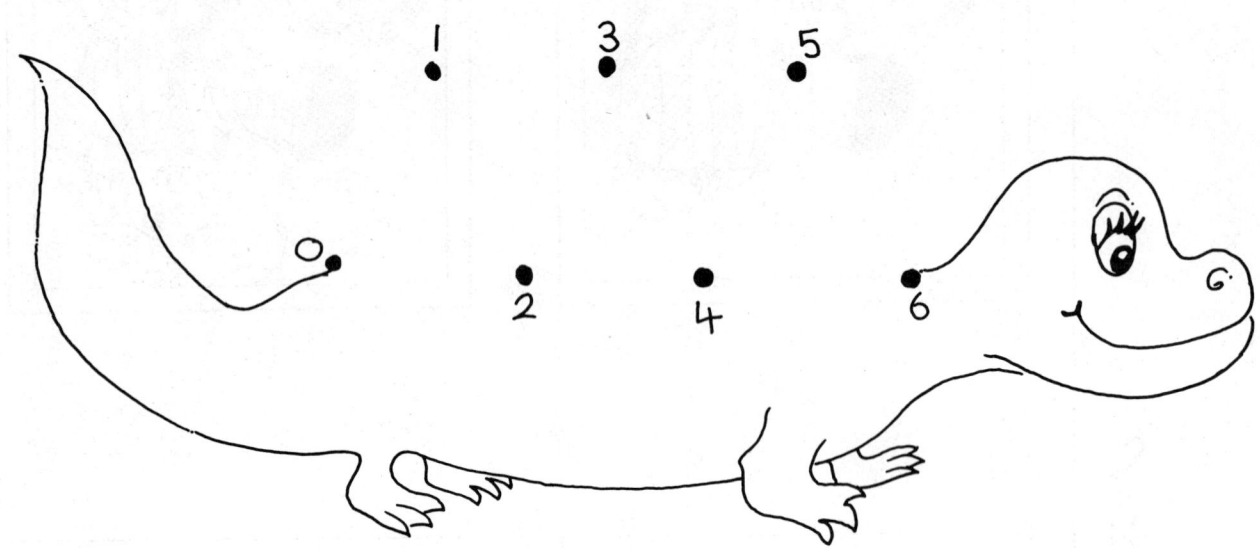

◆ ESSENTIALS FOR MATHS: Numbers to 9

 ─

◆ Name _____

Dotty toys – 2

◆ ESSENTIALS FOR MATHS: Numbers to 9

◆ Name _____

Dotty toys – 4

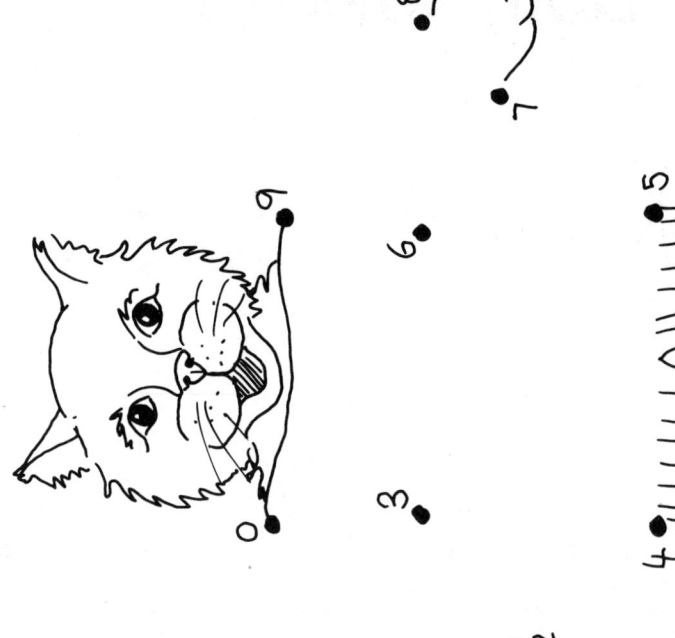
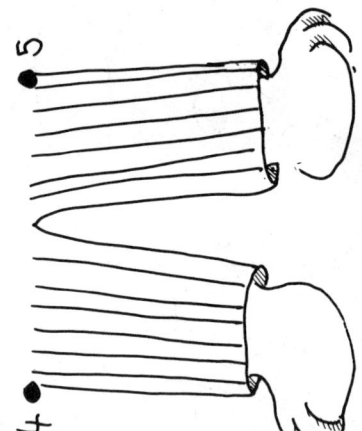

◆ Name _____

Dotty toys – 3

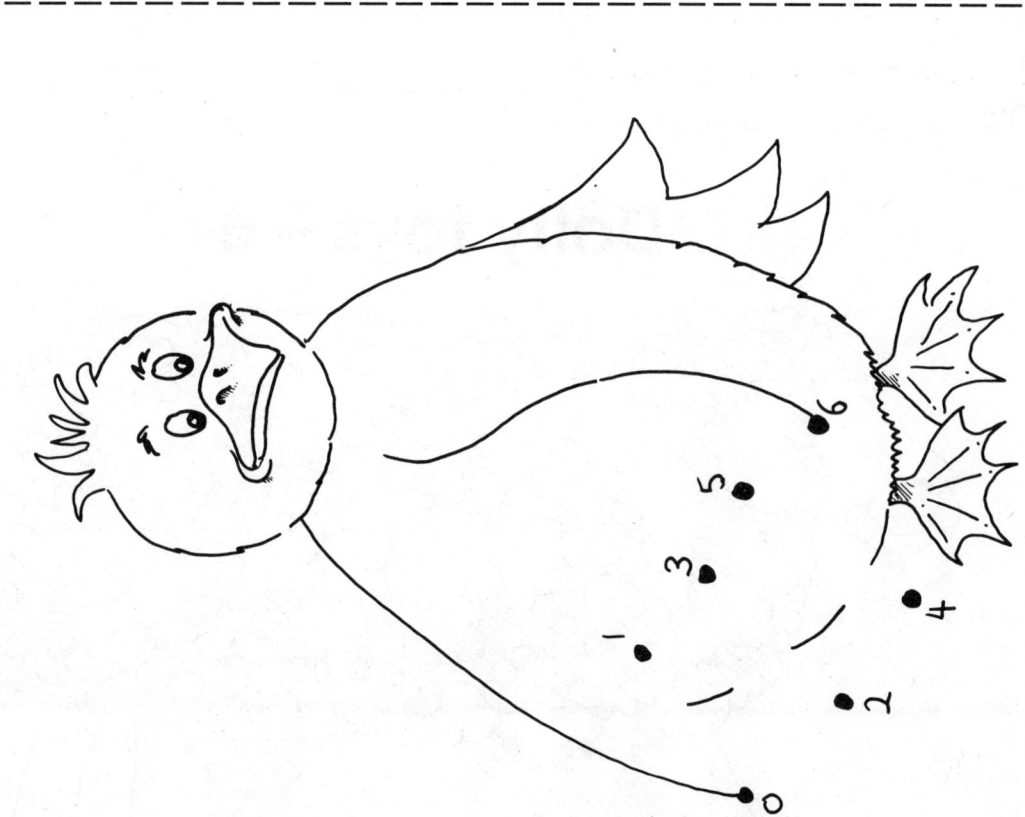

◆ ESSENTIALS FOR MATHS: Numbers to 9

◆ Name _____

Dotty toys – 5

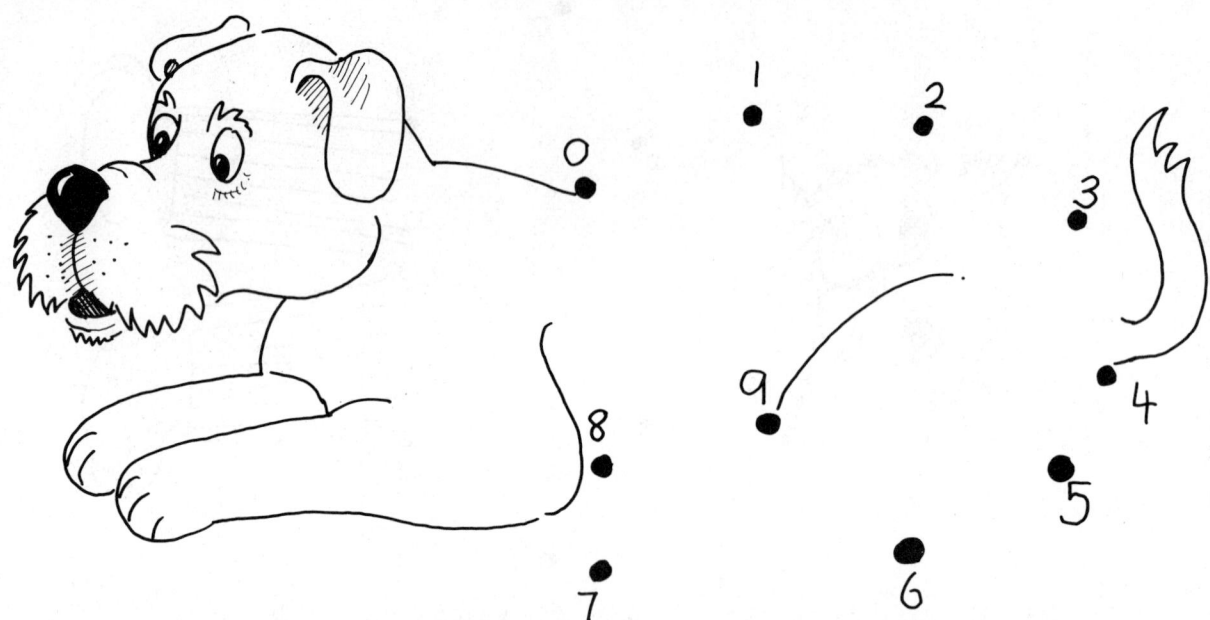

◆ ESSENTIALS FOR MATHS: Numbers to 9

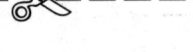

◆ Name _____

Dotty toys – 6

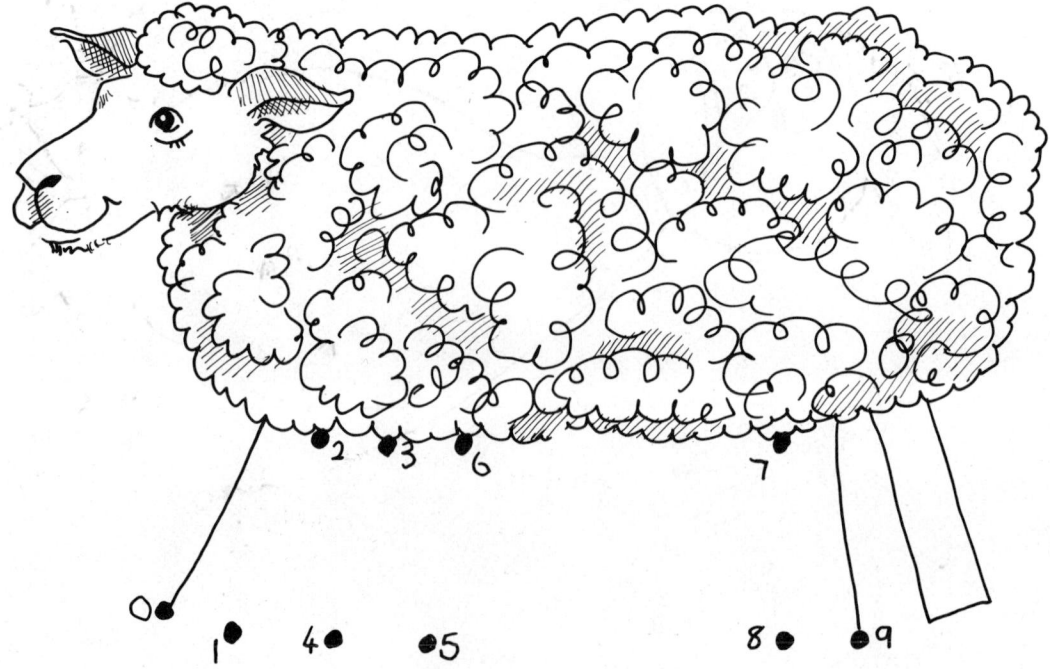

◆ ESSENTIALS FOR MATHS: Numbers to 9

20

Elephant counting cards

ESSENTIALS FOR MATHS: Numbers to 9

◆ Name _____

Stars

◆ Put ………… stars on each elephant.

◆ How many stars altogether?   □ + □ + □ = □

◆ ESSENTIALS FOR MATHS: Numbers to 9

◆ Name _____

Elephants in order

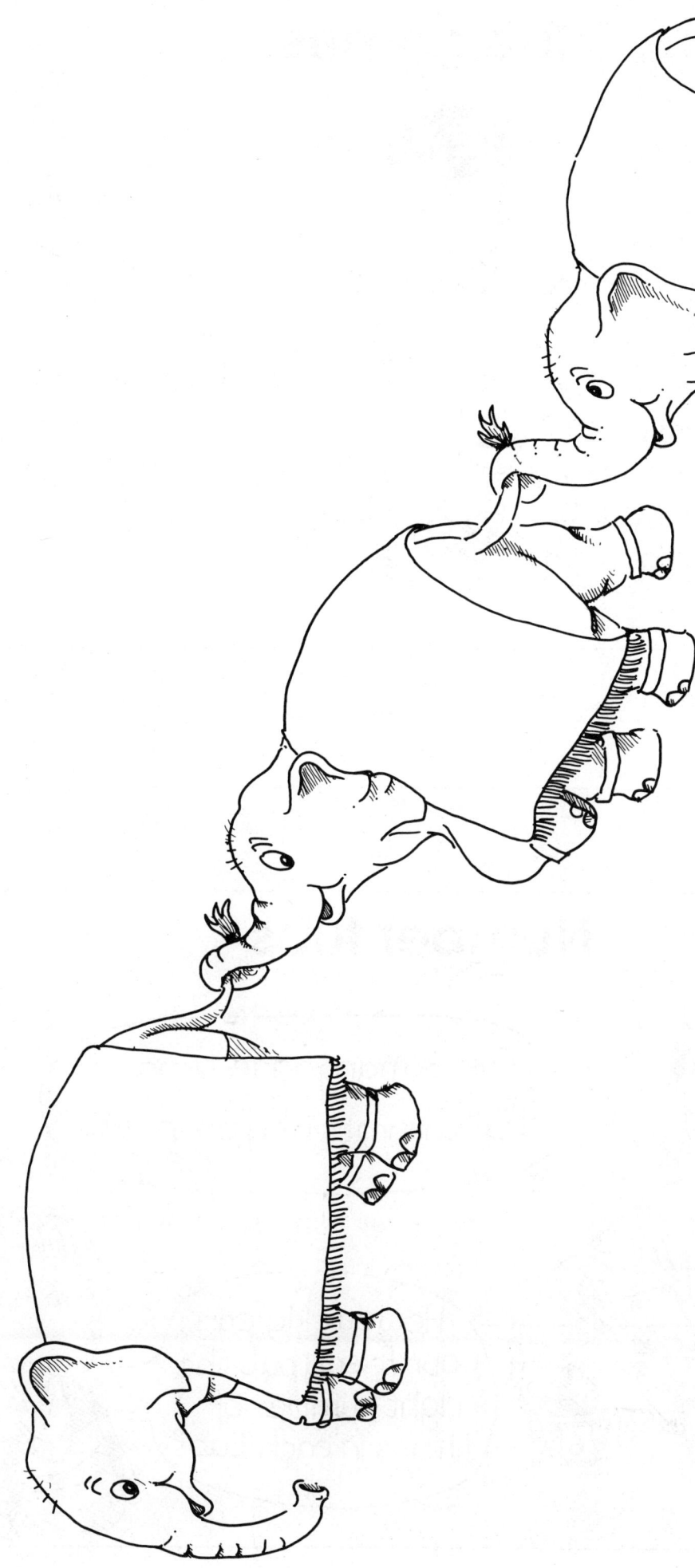

◆ Colour the elephants' blankets.
The 1st one is red.
The 2nd one is yellow.
The 3rd one is green.

◆ ESSENTIALS FOR MATHS: Numbers to 9

Tub games

Number tubs

Tubberly winks

◆ Play tiddly-winks. Choose a number to practise.

◆ ESSENTIALS FOR MATHS: Numbers to 9

Tub split-ups

◆ Choose a number to practise.

Hide-away tubs

◆ Choose a number to practise.

◆ ESSENTIALS FOR MATHS: Numbers to 9

Tub sums

◆ Make up a sum for your friend to do. Use a tub, like this:

◆ ESSENTIALS FOR MATHS: Numbers to 9

26

Parent's letter for 'tub games'

Stick a copy of your school letter heading over this,
before making copies to give to parents.
Don't forget to sign the letter!

Dear Parent,
    Your child has been playing some counting games at school, and we thought you might like to help by playing the games at home, too.
    The games are very simple. The booklet explains what to do for each one. I've sent a set of number cards for you to use, too, if you'd like to do this.
    Use anything your child is interested in to count with – small cars, plastic animals, conkers or marbles, for example. You will need two or three empty margarine tubs – or you could use plastic bowls or something similar.
    It's best to play just one or two of the games for a few minutes each day. To start with, your child might be happiest if you only use the smaller numbers (perhaps up to 5), and then gradually introduce 6, 7, 8 and 9 as your child becomes more confident.

    Thank you for your help,
    With best wishes,

    Class teacher

Tub sums – 1

"I put 2 marbles in my tub. Then I put in 2 more."

◆ How many marbles are in the tub? _____

◆ Check with a calculator.

☐ + ☐ = ☐

"I put 3 marbles in my tub. Then I put in 4 more."

◆ How many marbles are in the tub? _____

◆ Check with a calculator.

☐ + ☐ = ☐

"I put 5 marbles in my tub. Then I put in 3 more."

◆ How many marbles are in the tub? _____

◆ Check with a calculator.

☐ + ☐ = ☐

◆ ESSENTIALS FOR MATHS: Numbers to 9

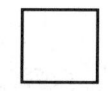

◆ Name _____

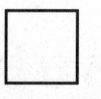

Tub sums – 2

◆ Make up some sums. Give them to your friends to try.

(Draw yourself here.)   (Write your friend's name here.)

_____ 's sum.

I put …… marbles in my tub.
Then I put in …… more.

◆ How many marbles are in the tub? _____

◆ Check with a calculator.

☐ + ☐ = ☐

(Draw yourself here.)   (Write your friend's name here.)

_____ 's sum.

I put …… marbles in my tub.
Then I put in …… more.

◆ How many marbles are in the tub? _____

◆ Check with a calculator.

☐ + ☐ = ☐

◆ ESSENTIALS FOR MATHS: Numbers to 9

◆ Name _____

Tub sums – 3

◆ Make up some take-away sums. Give them to your friends to try.

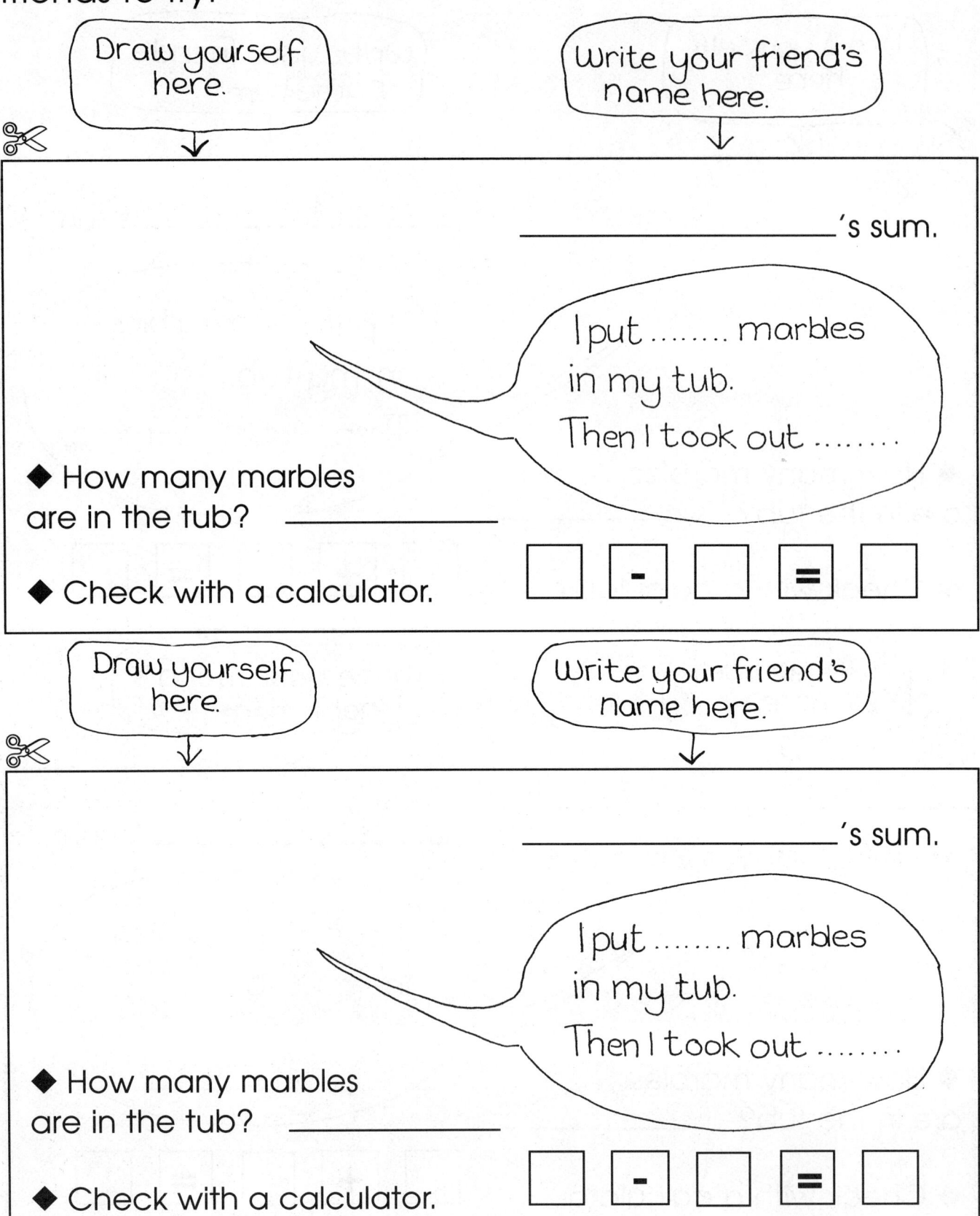

◆ Name _____

Birds

◆ Colour in the birds.
How many birds are sitting on the fence? _____

◆ Here's Cat! How many birds flew away? _____

◆ How many birds are left? _____

◆ ESSENTIALS FOR MATHS: Numbers to 9

◆ Name _____

More birds

◆ Make up your own story.
Draw some birds on the fence. How many birds are sitting on the fence? _____

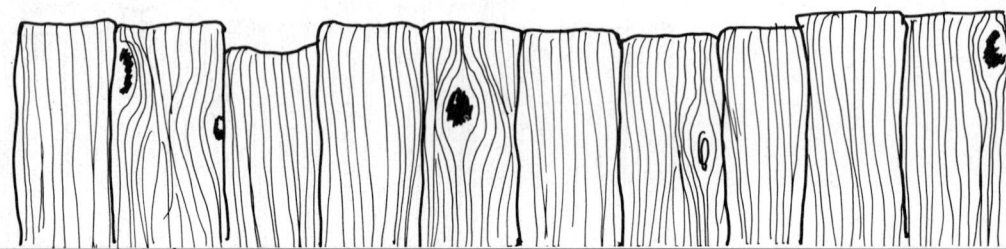

◆ Here's Cat! How many birds flew away? _____

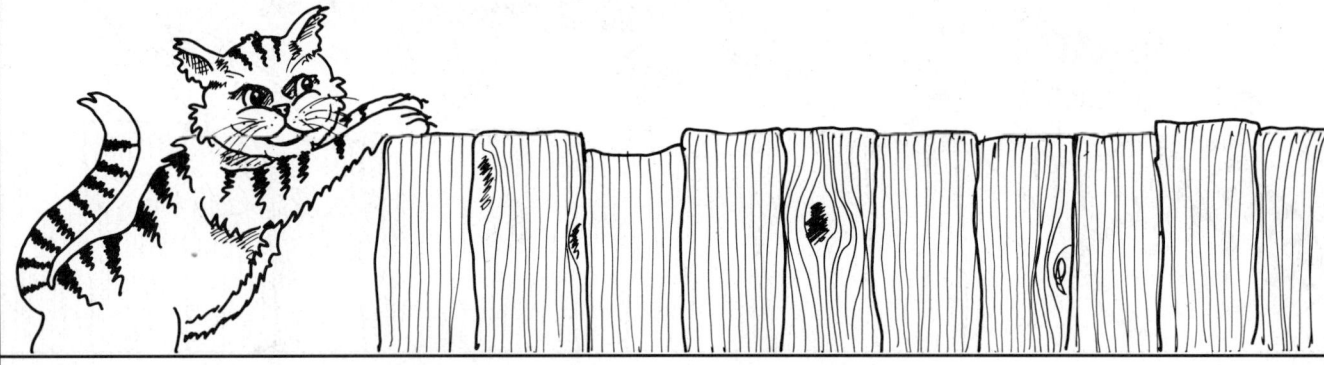

◆ How many birds are left? _____